The Light at the Edge of Everything

Anhinga Press

The Light at the Edge of Everything

Lisa Zimmerman

Poems

Anhinga Press
Tallahassee, Florida
2008

Cover Photo: John Zimmerman
Author Photo: Michele M. Barnett
Cover design, book design, and production: Dean Newman and C. L. Knight
Typesetting: Dean Newman
Type Styles: titles set in Minion Pro and text set in Weiss

Library of Congress Cataloging-in-Publication Data
The Light at the Edge of Everything by Lisa Zimmerman — First Edition
ISBN — 978-1-934695-03-6
Library of Congress Cataloging Card Number — 2008924707

This publication is sponsored by a grant
from the Florida Department of State
Division of Cultural Affairs, and the Florida Arts Council.

Anhinga Press Inc. is a nonprofit corporation dedicated wholly to the
publication and appreciation of fine poetry and other literary genres.

For personal orders, catalogs
and information write to:
Anhinga Press
P.O. Box 10595
Tallahassee, Florida 32302
Web site: www.anhinga.org
E-mail: info@anhinga.org

Published in the United States
by Anhinga Press
Tallahassee, Florida

For John

Contents

I

3   *Enough*

4   *The Dog and the Calling World*

5   *After I Buried My Father*

6   *River Rising*

7   *Forgiving My Father*

8   *Rain, Sleet, Snow and God*

9   *My Mother's Bedroom, My Mother's Closet*

10   *Sister, 1965*

11   *Shoes*

12   *Wings*

13   *View from the Castle Overlook*

14   *In the Beginning of Dangerous*

15   *Sudden Fiction*

16   *After Lightning*

17   *An Abbreviated Version of the Truth*

18   *Hillcrest Drive, Albuquerque*

20   *Karma*

21   *Unrecovered*

22   *Sestina for How Some Things End in the End*

24   *After Franz Wright*

25   *Releasing the Red-tail Hawk, Earth Day*

26   *Rain*

II

29   *Two Bowls*

30   *Winter Is Not*

31   *Kindergarten*

32   *Dog from the Original Fire*

33   *The Ring Around Us*

34   *November Drought*

35   *When I Worked in the Bookstore*

36   *After and Before the Seaquarium*

37   *Once Upon a Time in October*

38   *Two Cemeteries Far Apart*

39   *Threshold*

40   *For My Sister Flying to New Zealand*

41   *Religion*

42   *Valentine's Day*

43   *Remembering Nick*

44   *Photograph of an Old Marriage*

45   *Absence*

46   *Something Like Christmas*

48   *There's Nothing More to Be Said*

III

51   *First Book*

52   *Duvet*

53   *Photo of Three Boys, a Girl and a Horse*

54   *Not Waiting for the Movie*

55   *What Matters*

56   *Driving South on I-25*

57   *Before My Daughter Leaves Her Boyfriend and Goes Away to College*

58   *Checking On the Pregnant Mare*

59   *The Way of Dream Horses*

60   *Coyotes in the Ditch*

61   *The Poem I Didn't Write*

62   *Airing*

63   *Waiting for My Son to Call*

64   *Sonnet for the Lonely Cook*

65   *Reading Alone for Hours*

66   *Birthday*

67   *Five Meditations on Hair*

68   *Slow Courage*

69   *About the Author*

Acknowledgments

Thanks to the editors of the following publications in which these poems first appeared, some in slightly different form.

Atlanta Review: "After Lightning"
Birmingham Poetry Review: "Absence"
Bryant Literary Review: "Kindergarten"
Blue Unicorn: "Dog from the Original Fire"
Calyx: "The Dog and the Calling World"
Chattahoochee Review: "My Mother's Bedroom, My Mother's Closet"
The Colorado Lawyer: "November Drought"
Common Ground Review: "Airing"
Comstock Review: "Winter Is Not"
Concrete Wolf: "Sister, 1965"
The Cortland Review: "Birthday"
Descant: "What the Dolphin Knows"
Freshwater: "Enough," "View from the Castle Overlook," and "When I Worked at the Bookstore"
Gypsy: "Releasing the Red-tail Hawk, Earth Day"
The Kerf: "Hillcrest Drive, Albuquerque"
Lucid Stone: "Sudden Fiction"
The MacGuffin: "Two Bowls," and "Once Upon a Time in October"
Main Street Rag: "Driving South on I-25"
Matter: "Flying to New Zealand"
New Delta Review: "First Book"
Paper Street: "In the Beginning of Dangerous"
Poet Lore: "Forgiving My Father"
Portland Review: "River Rising," and "After Franz Wright"
Riverrun: "What Matters"
Rio Grande Review: "Threshold"
River Styx: "For Nick"
Tar Wolf Review: "Valentine"
Tryst: "The Ring Around Us," and "Rain"
Worcester Review: "Checking on the Pregnant Mare"

With gratitude to the poets who helped with this manuscript: Veronica Patterson, Jack Martin, Evan Oakley, Linda Aldrich, Melissa Katsimpalis, Robert King, Rick Campbell and George Kalamaras. Heartfelt thanks to Michele Barnett, Wendy Berger, Mary Greeley, my sister Diane, my husband John and my children Sylvan, Avalon and Arthur, for their deep support of my life and work.

Last night I dreamed I saw
God, and was talking to God
And I dreamed that God was listening…
And then I dreamed I was dreaming.

— Antonio Machado (tr. Alan S. Trueblood)

Everything begins by being dreamt.

— Marianne Boruch

The Light at the Edge of Everything

I

What is longing if not the ghost of memory?
— Helen Humphries

Enough

Dark, deliberate is how
you pull along the margin
of all my careful forgetting.
I don't think of you often
anymore when I thread a needle or fold a towel
or whip eggs into a happy froth.
Today the gardens are breaking
into chaos and light left over
at the end of the afternoon wants to prove
something about *root* and *possible*.
At seven I had been sad my whole life
yet I looked into the eyes of horses
and my one good grandmother
and saw this small house,
a green plate of water, a daughter
singing to the radio, a man who cooks dinner
and lets me spend hours with the pregnant mare
because a lot of women in my life died in April
and the sunlight fringing the crabapple tree
is enough.

The Dog and the Calling World

After Hurricane Katrina

A fox trotted along the fence last night
quick pad of black paws leaving
just enough scent in the dust holding
the dead grass in place for winter
that my dog finds the rusty smell
when he dives for the tennis ball.

I call his name but he devours
fox through his nostrils.
When thin clouds, finished at last
with their short sleep against the mountain,
leave the sky and fall like empty snow
onto the lake's green plate,
only then does the dog waken to my voice.

*

Later, asleep on a sheet of TV light,
his legs quiver and a muffled bark
escapes into the news-filled air. The screen
offers a parade of Southern dogs and cats
delivered at last by human hands
from their fled and sinking homes —
the silence of the drowned,
the starved, the four-legged.

In a different city, in a strange bed,
a child calls out in her sleep.
The dog, in a shelter, dreams her voice,
her hands with their scent of dirt and candy.
She is tugging his worn leash or throwing the ball
and he is leaping, leaping.

After I Buried My Father

the girl calls to say her dog was struck by a fast car.
I'm frying small circles of yellow squash in a pan, the phone
pressed against my ear. She is crying, bewildered, how
the car didn't even brake, didn't pull over to see
what creature was crushed against the curb.
The kitchen is steamy with onions and garlic,
Sinatra crooning from the other room.
She is sobbing, I say, *go ahead, every tear.*
On the back porch my own dog
lies in a thin river of moonlight.
I know she won't come to class the next day.
I say *you loved him.* He had a bright collar,
toys that squeaked, her hand sliding over the silk
of his black ears.

I visit the horses before bed.
Near midnight, all the neighbor dogs are quiet.
Even the moon weeps a path across the lake.
Geese open and close their wings along its shimmering border.

River Rising

Winter shrank into itself
so dry the peach tree came down
with one hatchet blow
and the mock orange beside
the bedroom window barely whispered

a fragrance.
Only today the iris fill
like purple cups with rain
and the river rises into pastures.
New foals lean, unsteady
against their mothers, quiet
beneath fronds of water,
their bodies heavy
with something —
how the world, to them,
gives and takes, gives
and takes, how easy it is
to bear it.

Forgiving My Father

I don't know if you have forgiven him, brother,
for keeping our house tight as a military barracks,
our beds pulled at the corners so snug a dime would bounce,
though we were not allowed to.
Outside in the dry heat of Albuquerque summer
you pushed the mower over grass
already standing at attention.

In the laundry room I opened the noisy dryer,
pulled out the dozen bleached handkerchiefs
with his three embroidered initials on the edge
and I starched them flat and folded them
and pressed the iron down again on each cotton square.

While our mother slept in a room with curtains
drawn closed against the day our father took
the sharpened clippers to the garage
and ran them over your head until you looked like him.
Afterwards I swept up your soft fair hair
and did not look at your sad boy's face or the dust
glittering in the air of the outside world.

Rain, Sleet, Snow and God

A thin March rain falls
on dry grass dreaming of snow,
my mares dark and wet.

I wake to a sleet
of what I didn't get done
on my whole week off

and wish the weather
channel had been right about
eight inches of snow.

As a girl I thought
God came from the sky as light.
Now I know better.

My Mother's Bedroom, My Mother's Closet

When the bedroom door stared shut before me
it could mean she was drunk again in the afternoon,
almost asleep, muttering beneath a polyester quilt.
Or it could mean she sat up in bed
reading a thick novel from the library stack
on her nightstand, and whatever it was
about me or the tilting universe, it could wait.

When the door swung ajar and my mother escaped
to the beauty parlor or the grocery store, I read
the backs of those books. In the hushed clutter
of her room, sunlight worked its dishwater rays
through the blinds. I learned from the words
on the book jackets, the other ways
she'd found to leave us.

And if the door fell open like a lonely heart
I crept into my mother's closet
and as silent as a lost girl can be, I slid
her exquisite Italian pumps from their tissued boxes —
touching the clean leather, the satin, the emerald brocade,
her silk dresses on their padded hangers brushing
the top of my head as I bent to each shoe, daring
my growing feet to slip inside.

Sister, 1965

I try to forget how autumn
creeps into us every year,
light drained to this cold blue November
where God placed you late in my childhood.
Kennedy was already dead and Dad
was on his way to Vietnam.
Not long until the house would fall
down inside itself —

Mom spidering toward the bottle,
the birch trees beyond the window
growing white with despair.

Shoes

My feet outgrew my mother's by the time I was twelve. She wore stilettos, floated from the house on my father's uniformed arm in a puff of Chanel #5. On Saturdays I polished my father's combat boots, using his fine brushes and cloth soft as skin. He wore those boots to Vietnam. He came home. The house could not walk away from anything. I waited for the prince with the glass slipper to save me.

Wings

Only two hummingbirds came to the feeder all summer though
I heard their whirring every day above the ash and aspens.
Bees drowned in the nectar, their cellophane wings coated with
sugar. Up at the barn a sparrow swept one wing too close to the
dangling fly paper, and it held. I cupped its body, felt the frantic
heart tapping against one hand while the other pried each silky
gray feather from the glue. Then I let it go.

View from the Castle Overlook

A village with cobblestone streets
bread baking in hidden ovens.

My brother is a saber.
My brother is an open window.

Do you see there is no curtain for it?
My sister is a violin. My father does not play

but buys it anyway from the antique shop
where he flashes his rude American money.

My sister is music drifting from the café.
My mother wants to stay at the little outdoor table

with her tall glass and its sweet liquor.
My father marches through all the torched cities.

He wants to visit the war cemeteries, every city —
all the graves. Walking fast so my mother gets thirsty.

I am a silk dress in the tailor's window.
My mother sees the blue from the corner of her eye.

In the Beginning of Dangerous

The first time a man put his tongue in my mouth
I was just twelve and he, at nineteen, rode a motorcycle
and smelled like work and dirt and beer and I felt
something fall down or maybe faint inside
my body somewhere under the breasts
I was imagining into a lacy white bra I might
have one day and whatever was fainting or falling there
kept getting up again to meet the movement of his warm lips,
his teeth clicking against mine, his tongue a sweet fish,
his hands pulled me closer, he thought
I was fifteen or sixteen, the party around us faded
and went out like a lamp as his fingers brushed along the edge
of my shirt, I felt his jeans tight
under my palms, I was rising and falling
and rising and falling and alive and aware
nothing really hard or terrible had happened to me yet.

Sudden Fiction

In the seeping twilight
bats find their way to trees
just beyond her doorstep.
She is washing something in the sink,
maybe carrots from the garden,
their hard slim bodies like the last
part of herself she's paring down and

he is just then looking up from his book,
his heart unfastened suddenly in his chest,
he fears the end, surely, at his age even this is possible,
the way she has reeled the marriage in like a net,
a filament, and he is outside
lost and rapidly falling.

After Lightning

For J.

I think of you each time I pass the tallest tree
beside the lake. It has to do with lightning,
how a streak cracked its whip so close
I froze inside its blind flash and the children
came racing from their rooms.
Later we found the tree, upright,
but with a deep tear from crown to root,
huge shards of bark thrown down
in the grass. Now when

I look at you, so many months since the death
of your son, I see the tree, the damp persistent wound,
the permanent bolt of white in your hair,
how it flowers in the dark.

An Abbreviated Version of the Truth

Leaning against hay bales, rain dripping
from the barn roof, the filly comes close,
sniffs my hair. I touch lightly
the small white flame on her forehead
amazed again how tall she's grown,
how her brown muzzle softens
all those years my father said
we couldn't buy a horse —
too many Army maneuvers
across oceans, continents.
Every horse I loved repaired
a broken piece of me.

Even the young thoroughbred gelding
who split my head open when I was ten —
concussion, thirty-three stitches, two black eyes.
The riding stable was fifteen miles from the military base.
I couldn't get back to him fast enough.

Hillcrest Drive, Albuquerque

There was the front walk, hot cement
leading past the pebbled landscape
a fringe of scratchy junipers
with their blue poison orbs.
There were the double front doors
of polished wood which might open
to a living room
where no one lived, arched
and obedient furniture matching
the imperious dining room table
whose water rings boiled
our mother to a rage.
There were sliding glass doors
along the concrete back porch
where we could see the neighbor's yard
and their small springing dog
on his thin tether
whom they surely loved more
than our parents loved us.
There was the fall of seventh grade
when mononucleosis wore me down
to utter nothing, closed my throat
and flung me into sweaty nightmares —
one where I saw my sleeping sister
sawed in half on wooden planks
by anonymous workers
in the neighbor's garden.
I fevered awake at dawn and stood
a long time staring through the paned glass
to the vacant day outside, everyone's yard
cool and quiet, the relentless New Mexican sun
not yet burning the day into submission.

And me, in a large empty house
all of thirteen and shivering
with a strangled swollen neck,
powerless to swallow my own spit.

Karma

I could love you once then let you go
alive in a life I cannot keep,
but I'd rather burn than die that slow.

Your hair, your breath, your eyes I know
from another time, some quantum leap
I could love you once then let you go.

A hundred years of wind could blow
the candles of the past asleep
but I'd rather burn than die that slow.

Beyond the meadow, beyond the glow
of sunlight brushing this hill of sheep
I could love you once then let you go.

The wreck of sex, the dive, the flow
into each other so true and deep
but I'd rather burn than die that slow.

To know you now, to want you so
I dream your ribs, your hands, I weep.
I could love you once then let you go
but I'd rather burn than die that slow.

Unrecovered

After 9/11

If the train came late and stood steaming on the tracks
If the children were arguing but you left on time
If taxis flew past even though your hand was raised
If a man bent down to pick up loose change
If the phone was ringing in an empty room
If the room was ringing in an empty mind
If ash has sifted to the back of your tongue
If the needle sings your name after all these years
If a bottle knows you better than the one who is missing
If they can't find a body, whose heart gets buried?

Sestina for How Some Things End in the End

We walked slowly through a sea of leaves,
the weather warm and voluptuous
while children shrieked and shouted on the playground
and baby strollers and dogs on leashes rushed beyond us.
Wind blew strands across your face
and I felt a small tragedy brewing.

Earlier we drank coffee, a black brew
and then you told me you were leaving.
The truth steamed from the cup to your face
the words in your mouth not sweet but voluptuous.
I didn't know what to think without us —
this college love reduced to an empty playground.

I could never hold my ground
with you and a storm in your eyes brewing.
So easy for you to think of yourself, not us,
not me, the bereft, the broken, the one you leave —
my heart squeezed, my grief voluptuous.
How I'll lie down alone in our bed and cover my face.

But while we walked through the park to the station, your face
showed you might not be finished with the moonlit playground
of our late night talks, the tears, the voluptuous
sex, the fresh and tangy brew
of our mismatched love. You kicked leaves,
like a kid. I took your hand. We were us.

And when the boy on the slide waved at us
you said he looked like your brother, that face
you miss every day, how sadness leaves
its singular dust on the very ground
of our being. And your eyes brew
their secret while clouds above the station float, voluptuous.

I just want time to hold its voluptuous
breath, to hold me, to hold us
in some eternal heaven for a moment, no brewing
weather, no grievous rain, only your lovely face
in my hands, me kissing you deep forever, to the ground
of who you are with me, who you will not be when you leave.

A sudden gust sent scattered leaves in a voluptuous arc.
They swirled around us and over the playground like last thoughts.
Our tragedy is brewed and blows, unforgiven, across your kissed face.

After Franz Wright

Nothing but a cube of city light yellow-white
like a rug on the floor beside the bed
where we are

Nothing but
blue neon flashing on your hip's slope
from the window see how
the sign wants you
as much as I want
this 2 a.m. to get inside
and rearrange all my
tired furniture

if I could smoke a cigarette
slow the way
I love your quiet
breathing beside me
there would be no
smoke, no ash,
no end to it

Releasing the Red-tail Hawk, Earth Day

She tossed him up
into that surprising rain
which fell on his healed wing
like kindness.
The gratitude was only human
as we watched him swoop and rise
and light easily on an upper branch
of the tallest cottonwood.

He was there when our cars
pulled away, birds darting in panic
below his silhouette
which was small at a distance
but clear and dark
and filled, like we are,
with power.

Rain

Yesterday I drove past a funeral,
dozens of people in sobbing light
and someone being lowered
into the sweet black dirt.
A man lifted his hands to his face.
I thought of my friend in the desert,
her firstborn buried in ground
which gives back nothing.

At home the lake surrenders, finally,
to the weather: a crushed gray sigh
floating the paired geese
like dark swans in an old story.

II

Oh what a glory it is that the winter snow
Should be so deep, that we know so little
And the future should be out of our hands!

— Robert Bly

Two Bowls

I don't know how it happened, the slip
of the first bowl, from my hands
into the sink.
The bowl with its clean lines of earth,
blue smoke abandoned to desert sky.
My mother nearby, crowding me,
her old anger, the splintered shards.
Something began to break,
I let go the bowl.

*

Sprigs of plum webbed the bottom,
a Japanese garden blown in glass,
this wedding bowl I lifted
from tissue and saw myself lift again
in twenty-five years. How we bring
what we love into the light
to keep us safe and inseparable.

*

From the couch my grandmother
called out the pieces of her past
just as I reached for the bowl, anticipation
of clarity, capacity to hold.
I felt the cool hard glass, how strong
we really are, how resilient, how
I would bury these two women
in darkness inside me
how the bowl shattered suddenly
and my feet bled.

Winter Is Not

the season of my birthday,
is not heat keeping the trees green
in the light, not sandals, or swimming
like a seal under the sky's blue arch,
not my white dog panting on the back porch
or my boy hiding in his leafy tree house.
Winter is not the day reaching its lavender branches
up to the moon's thin cradle, not my horses
standing head to tail in the shade
not sheets holding the afternoon
in their cotton weave or geese clucking softly
through the screen, not the fireflies
of my broken childhood, not my daughters' bare
shoulders or lemonade in a clear glass or your cool hands
finding me awake in the careful dark.

Kindergarten

It's hard to know
how much they love their children,
these mothers and fathers
reaching across a five-year-old lap
to unlatch the car door,
or holding that mittened hand
block after block to the brick school
with its slide and gravel, the teacher
with her impossible smile.
Because at the same moment somewhere
a child is being beaten by a parent who was beaten
by a parent who was locked in a basement.
It's hard to tell
when you watch a woman
bend down to kiss her small child
what hurts most, in which family, on whose body.

Dog from the Original Fire

I have a German Shepherd
the sheriff's department would love
for his giant chest, his hundred and twenty
pound frame, his desire for honest work.

He helps me feed the horses,
rummages for mice behind the grain bin.
When the mares get pushy his bark
booms across the frozen lake
and foxes slink away in their thin red sleep.

The growl from his throat
is prehistoric, a rumble from a black cave
where firelight breaks the rock in tattered shadows.
He knows there is danger in the world, and fear
is neither influence nor abstract.

When the doorbell sings its one chime
he looms quiet on the other side.
Being ready is a solemn job. He could do it forever.
In the cave of his ribs his heart is an ember.

The Ring Around Us

A sudden gust of wind on the rim of sleep
Waking seeds ticking in the bird feeder
Where soft green wings in the river limbs rustle
Pale light of finches halos the elm tree

Waking seeds ticking in the bird feeder
And the bones of the young fox buried beyond
Pale light of finches halos the elm tree
Ghost of a good dog and three silky cats

And the bones of the young fox buried beyond
At the edge of the yard with its ribboned grass
Ghost of a good dog and three silky cats
A necklace of creatures stirs the soil

At the edge of the yard with its ribboned grass
What we love fringes the hem of our slumber
Where soft green wings in the river limbs rustle
A sudden gust of wind on the rim of sleep

November Drought

Where the highway pulls its belt of ash
between the hammered winter fields,
a hawk shares the wasting twilight
with branches empty as thoughts.

A rancher, weighed down by his blue jacket,
looks across his sea of sheep, wheat-colored
against the cracked grass. Beside him, his dogs turn
like two black and white wheels.

At the salon in town his wife
lies down naked on the tanning bed.
Wind blows the hawk into open sky.
The dogs pant, waiting for directions.

The man stares across the knobs of wool.
His face is hewn silver; his heart, gravel.
The horizon is dry, boned and narrow,
with rain remote and unlikely as tears.

When I Worked in the Bookstore

The unbuckled light in the car
when the door opens to winter dusk —
the dog leaning against the black fence
as we pull away like tidewater
from our house by the lake.

Every year pares down to this
starved light squeezed through
the tiny aperture at the end
of December. Christmas is
the garbled message

on the answering machine,
pins of bright color strung
on empty tree branches,
the child in the bookstore sobbing,
A book, Daddy, please a little book,

beside the divorced and angry man
who cannot bear another minute of tinsel
or angel cards or me coming up the broad green
staircase with something small and inexpensive
in my hands.

After and Before the Seaquarium

What the dolphin knows
can't be phrased with a dry tongue,
and they never did say what
she knows, only that
she is not apparently unhappy;
after all, freedom is a state of mind.

How the tide of applause buoys her up
in a magnificent arc, dreaming
of ocean, blue curve of bliss:

how when they dragged her up
from her indigo life
she felt the weight of her body
for the first time —
an ancient sorrow, lost speech
of captivity.

Once Upon a Time in October

It rattled in the corn today
shaking itself inside the leaves,
I heard it as I moved the new baby
into light falling between the branches.
For a moment all I wanted
was to stand in that brittle light
and listen to carrots burrow
deeper into soil and hold
the baby sleeping against me,
his head a warm peach, the soft
spot a bruise against my lips
where God still speaks into him,
promising all things: a life
rich in love and sorrow.
And when the bones close,
my son will remember nothing
but a distant wind, a murmur
in the leaves.

Two Cemeteries Far Apart

There was a time I didn't think of death
in the cemetery in wavering summer light,
water with its little fall from the fountain
to the pond floating two swans.
The dead are still dead
on this hill where I sat years ago,
my daughters setting pink and yellow plastic ponies
against the chiseled headstones, my baby boy
napping on a blanket in the shade of old trees.
Trucks from the nearby quarry still creep
along the road with their gravel loads
and a rumble of purpose carries over the graves.
The living are so busy.

*

At my father's funeral soldiers carry
his gray casket under a canopy
that keeps February's new sun
high above us. My mother's white
headstone has been plucked
from the ground like a tooth
and leans against an empty chair
to make room for her husband.
Soldiers will give it back to the earth
later in the windy morning
after everything is said,
everything done.

Threshold

Between the sun and the spool
This unraveling
Between the God and the wine
This white absence
Between the moment and the miracle
A prolonged panic
Between the wish and the weeping

For My Sister Flying to New Zealand

For us it's morning, smell of coffee
rising in an orbit where we feel
the jet pulling you west,
you belted inside the sleek metal bird
shearing through these hours like water.

Time is unraveled by speed
as you fly across the thin threads
circling the world but at home
it's purring through rooms, lifting
children out of beds, making space
for the day's countless small jobs.
While a net of snow feathers the yard
we almost hear you step from our side of things —

already tomorrow, already summer.

Religion

I believed in the witnessing angel
even as my mother feared God
and loved gin.
I saw the wavering candle in the black room
when my eyes slid behind
each worried dream of childhood.

I did not hate the people who harmed me.
I took that sorrow like grain
and ground it down
under each weighted day
and made a loaf and let it rise
and let it rise
into the heated hours.

Every day I break off a piece
of this bread and offer it
to the angel who sits behind me,
the one who travels through
the terrible night forest while I sleep,
silently raking through the trees.

Valentine's Day

Behind the house is a secret
bedding down in the dry lace
of winter grass.
Three deer sleep
beneath night's dark affection.
The small notes of their hoof prints
leave a message, like a letter
that you discover one late afternoon
as you carry a single rose
to your neighbor, the woman
with cancer's black candy flower
beginning to break open
on her forehead.

Remembering Nick

Even now the gale howls from the sea to your farm,
lifting grass up to your window,
rushing through leeks and lettuce in your garden.
I can't hear it but I know you are listening.

Somewhere near that shore
where our feet gripped gray rock through our shoes
as the tide receded slowly toward Wales,
somewhere this night
seagulls stand on those wet stones where we walked.

I can see you now in your trembling house
the dogs asleep and warm on your lap,
how the wind was everywhere that day
except between our clasped hands.

Photograph of an Old Marriage

When their daughter's wedding reception clatters happily
out of range they pose, shoulder to shoulder,
in the bulb's brief flash. And isn't that it?
Their own marriage deep

yet fleeting, children flying up
into singular struggles, the cake sweet
between his fingers which will undo
the buttons of her ivory dress

later when they are both tired,
the rose on his lapel
browning.
Again shoulder to shoulder

their bones older, yes,
but the bed a small harbor
and the sugar of the afternoon
still on their lips.

Absence

He was a bright guy but a punk really, a smirking kid
at the back of the room. A sweet talker. Dark
hair and eyes and a boyish smile.
Days went by where I called his name
and the other kids just shook their heads.
We wrote a lot of paragraphs. There was a war
in Iraq. One afternoon he appeared
at my office. Jail time and his mom not bailing.
He came back to class for a couple of weeks.
He wrote about wanting to become a teacher. He couldn't
fuck up again or there would be serious prison time.
I let him use the word fuck in his essays.
His writing was otherwise clear
and steady. I told him I'd do what I could.
He disappeared before the last week of the semester.
I had to give him a D. For disappointment.
For decision. For disappeared.

Something Like Christmas

It takes an abused woman an average
of five times to finally leave her husband.

Christmas eve and a thread
of blood on the plate,
dinner steaming in sorry piles.
One tooth moves a little
when her tongue briefly touches.
The police come and she pulls
the oldest child close, knows
the thump her heart makes
against his ear while they ask
and ask until she thinks
the house is not broken but shaped
like the answer, a bruise just blooming
inside her ribs. She gathers
her work shirt, her apron, a few things
to live through the next day.

> The safe house is crowded
> with fractured families, jaws wired
> into whisper, lips sewn time after time —
> women counsel her and say
> what will happen if she shuttles
> her children like bundled laundry
> into their rooms again, the *ssh he's sleeping*
> followed by a swift scrubbing of the kitchen,
> the new day cracked open like a yard of broken glass.

She thinks of the wrapped gifts
beneath the tree, how to go back
so her kids will have something
like Christmas.
The house is a smudge, a dark heartbeat
in the middle of the street,
guns shiny and asleep in the bedroom,
every blinking red light on the tree
a tiny silent ambulance.

There's Nothing More to Be Said

for this crooked glass moon
leaning its clean blue arms
across the backs of these horses.

III

Each day
the same sun
climbing its bright stairs.

— Joe Survant

First Book

after a question from my poetry class

When the designer asked me
how long it took to write the book
I said, *Twenty years.* So how
the waiting became a landscape of days
weaving their dark and bright threads
along the curious hem of my impatience
is perhaps more than I can say.

Each month that soared off the calendar
like a kite in a brisk wind left me
with another cluster of images that were not
in the book: an empty house from childhood,
a daughter in love and weeping, a boy tall
and so sinewed we cannot feed him enough
in the hours between the school he hates
and the martial arts that carve him
toward manhood.

My mother was still dead when April
opened its leafy pockets and the lake quietly
asked to be on the cover, but the mare
and foal grazed easily along the shore in June
and are lavendered forever on the glossy black page.
September finds me standing here before you
like a woman pregnant in middle age —
astonished, the unsaid poem in my mouth.

Duvet

Outside the window
wrens and sparrows fill
our pillows.

Too hot, we shift on cotton,
three-hundred thread count
no breeze in the weave.

Gold leaves scatter
October bright as copper.
Your warm legs near mine,

green sea foam
floats over our sleeping —
snow can't enter here.

Photo of Three Boys, a Girl and a Horse

The simple way children have
of becoming still and thoughtful
between rampant burst of play.
The sky behind them is white and endless.
What passes quietly through their minds?
Our eyes travel like spiders
up the slope of grass
just before the girl mounts the bay mare
and rides out of the picture, before
the boys shuffle back
to their invisible bases and wait
for the ball to race through the air
toward them
like time.

Not Waiting for the Movie

If you could dream your way back
to the galloping past with its weather and mystery
who would you drag again to your bed,
to its rucked up sheets, its cotton Indian throw?

*

In the library's papered fluorescent hush
you could hear blood thickening
beneath the skin's page.
What you really wanted was to love
the whole book, love the story inside the body,
the strange dangerous narrative.

How distracted you were, how disappointed
by indifferent angular boys, by late night
coffee and beer, talk turning over
its poverty and secrets, unrevealed.

Who knew he would find you, finally?
Both of you wandering in lives paragraphed with longing
filled with fragments, ravenous and willing
to read to the end.

What Matters

I never guessed when you arrived
that elephants would amble so suddenly
toward extinction. I didn't hear
the breath of the planet
wheeze through the hole
above Antarctica; I so loved
the small solid armor of your chest,
your serious face, your acceptance
of the life you thought I made for you.

At six you were a soldier, solemn
and directed as you lifted a drowning worm
from the gutter and placed it safely
in the garden mud.
I watched you from the porch, rain glazing
that afternoon, that gesture, and I felt
a dolphin burst free from the net
on the other side
of the world.

Driving South on I-25

white car swift as thought
down the black glass highway,
the doomed roar of trucks passing
in their quick haze, petals of exhaust
huffing over the stubbled gold.

A dark hawk flies thin above this string
of metal bullets speeding over asphalt,
dip and slide on a shoulder of wind.
I catch a glimpse through the window —

weight of rubber and steel in the pit
of my body, my body in the pit of the car —

never the whole delight of bird, of flight.

Before My Daughter Leaves Her Boyfriend
and Goes Away to College

I want to tell her it might not last,
this love with its thorns and kisses,
its fragrant heat, its window heart.

Summer. Peaches ripen
in a luminous bowl. The moth orchid
on the table drops a purple bloom.

In her narrow bed they sleep deep
into the day. Her arm
across his tattooed chest.

His cheek against her pale shoulder.
"Wake the children," I say to the dog,
because they are.

Checking on the Pregnant Mare

Sleep navigates the tides of time
— Dylan Thomas

Up and out of the boat, our bed
with the clock's orange ticking,
to slide into clothes and not wake you.
Because of night's travelers — skunk and fox —
the dog stays in as I unlatch the gate
and walk along a spring moon's narrow river
to the barn.

Two mares, one white as bone beneath
an uneven splash of stars, the other
dark in the breathing stall.
No light but the moon's liquid hum
and the large movement of the mare on straw
slowly eating supper's last hay at 1 a.m.

In the hammock of her belly the foal
on silent waves of sleep
hears the moon beckon
and answers back
not yet, not yet.

The Way of Dream Horses

The way dawn eased upward from the soil, wet and silver
The way I slept deeply beyond the 3 a.m. alarm
Night lifted like a bird of smoke
You sat up in bed and said, *I dreamed there was a foal*

The way I slept deeply beyond the 3 a.m. alarm
You pulled on shorts and ran across the yard
The way you sat up in bed and said, *I dreamed there was a foal*
I quickly gathered clothes when you told me it was true

The way you pulled on shorts and ran across the yard
Breath burned my lungs as I raced to the barn
After throwing on my clothes when you shouted it was true
The foal was darkness on a nest of straw

How my breath burned my lungs when I entered the barn
The slow and careful way you knelt down to her body
The way the foal was darkness on a nest of straw
How she scrambled up, all legs and ears and tail

Careful, you knelt and gently touched her body
How the mare nickered low and moved toward her in the barn
The way she scrambled up, all legs and ears and tail
Day broke open beyond fences and sky

The mare nickered low and we were quiet in the barn
Night lifted like a bird of smoke
Then the day broke open beyond fences and sky
And dawn eased upward from the soil, wet and silver

Coyotes in the Ditch

Sometimes in summer we wake
to their high-pitched chorus
carried across the rope of sleep.
Night sky abates and becomes
pasture, becomes singing —
horses stir and rustle,
the moon's white fangs pierce
chinks in the barn.

When you tell me you listened
to a pack in full daylight
take an animal down, bone by bone
in the snowy ditch —
we imagine a February calf
as the prize, imagine
the tender throat exposed.
All day you couldn't shake
that gleeful barking.

Tonight the farmer's cows across the road
low endlessly, their calves vanished
into the dark interior of trucks at dawn.
Beyond the string of fence the coyotes
begin their refrain.

The Poem I Didn't Write

In the poem I didn't write are all the seedlings
scorched by weeks of no rain and the riot
in the garden we name daisies
and the silver shepherd fur
lining the nest hidden in the hay barn.
The poem I didn't write has room for the barbed
wire fence tangled in dry brush
and my careful step aside and the fox panting
in the shade of one alfalfa bush at the top
of the farm road.
The unwritten poem keeps time
with a boy in the house whose muscles ache
from long nights of Kung Fu and the sister
who wears inked scissors on her leg.
The poem listens to the news and Syrian missiles
and refuses to speak about the stitches
sewn at dusk by the old vet on the young mare's leg
or how she had dragged broken wooden fence
behind her with all its terrible shards and nails.
And the poem finds no syntax for the beating heart
of a U.S. Army M.D. in Iraq who wipes his face
with a shaking hand and says, *It's not a good day
to be a doctor, not here.*

Airing

black trousers choked by slow water
slack sleeves regret the pin, the line
on the fence a sheet in sun
   everything empty,
      everything even —

a damp dog, large, drying in the yard
horses, hidden by an arm of shade
dusky lake, not one crease
   grief was not
     what she meant —

the great white egret
like a white nightgown
on a branch high above the water
   look,
     how the day is —

the easy breath, the sweet green
light at the edge of everything

Waiting for My Son to Call

A thin moon shines fierce and fragile
above the row of fragrant pies.
I haven't been to Perkins
since my grandmother
sat across from me, delighted
by her cherry pie á la mode
and enchanted by my boy who is now
taller than I am with the faint
whisper of a mustache.

My grandmother told me she only wanted to live
long enough to hear her great-grandson read,
and she did. Right now
he is sitting with a serious girl
whose long brown hair swept
down her slim back as he followed her
up the stairs to study in her room.
From the car I looked at the square of light
that was her window or the bright new page
in a story they are reading
and writing at the same time.

Sonnet for the Lonely Cook

A ring of flame flickers blue under the iron pot,
the broth lifting into a simmer and steam
clouding the kitchen window, the knot
of garlic softening amid carrots, onions, the gleam
of the spoon in my hand as I think
about my mother, gone this long decade.
In the autumn-strewn yard beyond the sink
and beyond the misted window day fades
to early dusk and the old sadness stirs
the fragrant soup. How she loved
to cook but ate so little in the end. Her recipes blur
on their index cards. The worn cookbooks move
with my sister from country to country, town to town.
Tonight in our separate kitchens we remember her, alone.

Reading Alone for Hours

Afternoon's last light pours its pale gold
behind the house and not through the window
where your head bends to a book filled

with the red silk poetry of Imperial Chinese women.
Each one stitched her calligraphy, her longing
tight and black as iron around her bound feet.

The minutes close their eyes and you call me.
All the women's loneliness and sorrow has entered

you who sit alone beneath evening's darkening glass.
And I say get up, daughter,
brew a steaming cup of ginger tea.

Then walk out in your bare feet
across the reassuring grass
that will rise up again behind your footprints.

Birthday

for John

On the edgeless map of the reliable world
a man stands on the star
that is his house, his garden
unfurling in open fans — small blue prayer
of forget-me-nots, raspberries leaping
in the vine's imagination, fists of peony
promising their red abandon.

It is the porous border of summer,
mirage of trees, clouds
floating like years over the mountains.
He has traveled far in his heart
to come to this full quiet
to witness weather stepping
across the lake toward him
like an ordinary saint bringing the news:
another whole day, loved.

Five Meditations on Hair

1.
My first-born daughter's bald head crowned
in the slate room before dawn
though hours would climb down the stairs of my body
before she emerged whole, glistening.
In high school she would dye her long hair black
because being blonde was overrated.

2.
The second daughter shaved half her head
when the P.E. teacher confessed to class
she had breast cancer. Two years later that daughter
shaved off all of her abundant red hair and I said
not beautiful. And I thought *Dachau.*

3.
My boy's first haircut was at age two.
He had curls. They fell like pale feathers
beneath the girl's swift scissors.

4.
When my son was fourteen I showed him
all the gray hair in my bangs.
He said *It looks like tinsel.*
Last August he got his head buzzed for Kung Fu.
He looked like a Marine. I say, *The war in Iraq
cannot have him.*

5.
The filly is as tall as the mare. They stand together
against the fence like sisters. I comb her long black tail.
Tucked inside, near the bottom, is a black corkscrew
of hair. It is the first tail, the one she was born with.

Slow Courage

For days in my head I kept hearing
the word *burden* but I wake again
and again not carrying anything
except a little emptiness
the swallows in the barn
fly in and out of.

Looking across the lake I know
my parents were gone long before
I felt the slow courage that carries us
weightless to the next year.

Yesterday my husband pointed to a blur
in the field and said *fox*
but dusk had taken all the colors
into its dark mouth and I had to conjure red
from my own heart.

About the Author

Lisa Zimmerman's first book, *How the Garden Looks from Here*, won the Violet Reed Hass Poetry Award and was published by Snake Nation Press. She is also the author of two chapbooks: *In Places Without Time Nothing Hurries* (Leaping Mountain Press), and *Traveling Among the Animals* (Pudding House Publications). She has been nominated twice for the Pushcart Prize. Her poetry and fiction have appeared in the *Colorado Review, Redbook, Atlanta Review, Portland Review, Indiana Review* and other journals. Zimmerman grew up in a military family, graduated from S.H.A.P.E. American High School in Belgium and received her MFA from Washington University in Saint Louis. She teaches composition and creative writing at the University of Northern Colorado and lives in nearby Fort Collins.